Poc...e.

Researcher...lder

Contents

Introduction 4

Tenerife at a Glance 6

History 8

Places of Interest 10

Coastal Resorts 17

Santa Cruz 20

Puerto de la Cruz 22

Touring by Car 24

When to Go 46

How to Get There 46

Insurance 47

Passport and Customs 47

Food and Drink 48

Telephone 49

Postal Service 49

Accommodation 49

Toilets 49

Electricity 50

Water 50

Holiday Reading 50

Photography 50

Weights and Measures 51

Money Matters 52

Police 53

Robbery 53

Medical Help 53

Island Transport 54

Sea Routes 55

Useful Words and Phrases 56

Sports and Entertainment 58

Excursions 62

Festivals and Fairs 64

Introduction

Tenerife is the largest of the seven islands which form the Islas Canarias or Canary Islands. To the Romans they were the Elysian Fields, to the Greeks they were the Garden of the Hesperides, where the golden apples of the sun grew. They are still considered heavenly today. Similar in latitude to the Bahamas, and blessed with a really beautiful climate, Tenerife, of all the islands, is now one of Europe's most popular holiday resorts – a sub-tropical paradise, rich in its flora and remarkably varied in its landscape. The coast of Africa and the Sahara Desert lie a mere 320km/200m to the east; the Tropic of Cancer is just a few degrees to the south. Trade winds warm the air above and the Atlantic Gulf Stream raises the temperature of the water around its shores. Not surprisingly, the Canaries have been known for centuries as the Fortunate Islands.

Spanish-speaking and Spanish in its appearance and outlook, Tenerife, nevertheless, has its own special character. And the same can be said for the other islands in the archipelago: La Gomera, La Palma, El Hierro, Gran Canaria, Lanzarote and Fuerteventura. Different people will find in each of them something special which appeals to them and draws them to its particular shores. The appeal of Tenerife is that it combines so many of these features in the one island. It is only a little over 2000 sq.km/1250 sq.m in area but, in that small space, manages to present the fortunate traveller with almost every type of scenic display: a magnificent mountain range, topped by an extinct volcano – Mount Teide, Spain's highest mountain at over 3700 m/12,000 ft – surrounded by a lunar-like landscape, hot arid regions, cool pine forests, lush green pastureland, exotic flowers throughout the year and, it seems, bananas as far as the eye can see.

So, for the visitor, there is a little of everything – a beautiful coastline, largely unspoilt throughout its length; some lovely old towns, full of character; small villages, simple in their appeal; new resorts where no effort has been spared to satisfy the tourist's every need; a delightful countryside; and an excellent road system by which to see it all.

Tenerife at a Glance

The island divides naturally into two parts, offering the visitor a clearcut choice between the green and fertile regions of the north and the dry, sun-baked south. Mount Teide (*MR* D5) and its chain of mountains are the reason for this sharp contrast between the two areas. Like a huge backbone, the range extends across the middle of the island as far as the northeastern tip, forming a cloud barrier, so that the majority of the rain tends to fall on the northern side.

Dominating the northeastern coastal strip is **Santa Cruz** (*MR* J2), the island's capital and largest town – the administrative, commercial and cultural centre of Tenerife. A charming city, liberally provided with shops, cafés, bars and restaurants, museums and churches, parks and open spaces in which to relax and a huge square looking out onto the harbour, where all the world can meet. A little further up the coast is **Playa de Las Teresitas** (*MR* K2) claimed to be the largest man-made beach in the world. A few miles inland you'll find the old capital of **La Laguna** (*MR* J2), a university town, rich in historical associations. The northern airport and several other nearby towns make this by far the most densely populated region in the island.

A little to the west lies one of the main red wine-producing areas, based in the town of **Tacoronte** (*MR* G2), extending almost as far as the beautiful resort of **Puerto de la Cruz** (*MR* E3). Puerto, as it is often known, lies midway along the north coast – a seductive place, full of charm and with numerous attractions, including the vast lido, a huge recreation park with separate pools. To the south is the **Orotava Valley** (*MR* F4) – a fertile plain reaching to the foothills of Mount Teide.

The middle of the island is entirely mountainous, green and lush in its northern reaches, becoming more barren as one approaches Mount Teide and the remarkable moonscape of **Las Canadas National Park** (*MR* D5).

On the south coast are the major resorts of **Playa de Las Americas** (*MR* C8) and **Los Cristianos** (*MR* C8) fast becoming the island's prime tourist centres, served by the southern airport only minutes away. Much of the land around has a parched look, but in the towns flowers grow in profusion, fed by water from the mountains and in the countryside, palm trees and cacti provide their own touch of the tropics. Tenerife, with its towns, villages and varied landscape seems able to offer the traveller a little of everything.

Traditional wooden balconies near Orotava (MR F3)

History

Little is known of the early history of the Canary Islands. The result of volcanic eruption long ago, they have been the subject of some fanciful theories as to their origins. Inevitably, the legend of Atlantis has found a place amongst them, since the lost civilisation was thought to have existed somewhere to the west of Gibraltar, in the area occupied by these islands.

Recorded history really begins in the 15th century when an expedition from Spain reached these islands, although there is evidence that others had travelled here earlier. At this time, the islands were occupied by a white-skinned, blue-eyed, fair-haired race. This unlikely colouring led some people to think that they must have come from Scandinavia, but all the evidence suggests that they originated in North Africa – from a group known as *Cromagnon* man. The intriguing thing is that, whilst they must clearly have arrived by sea, no remains of any boats have been discovered.

On Tenerife, the natives were known as Guanches. They were cave-dwellers, without knowledge of metal; herdsmen who grew cereals for food. When the Spanish arrived at the beginning of the 15th century, these aborigines were still in the stone age. But they did posses one unexpected skill – they mummified their dead in the manner of the Egyptians, wrapping the bodies in goats' skins and matting. From where they learnt the art is a mystery.

Some of the islands welcomed the new colonisers, but on Tenerife they resisted bitterly and with great bravery. It was not until 1496, nearly 100 years after the Spanish first arrived, that they were finally overcome. Four years earlier, *Columbus* had stopped at Gran Canaria on his way to discovering the new world.

In a comparatively short space of time, the islands became totally Spanish – never as colonies, but completely integrated as part of Spain. Sugar, malmsey wine, cochineal and bananas all played their part in their economic development. Although a number of European countries cast covetous eyes in their direction, none of them succeeded in taking control anywhere. In 1797, Nelson attacked the garrison at Santa Cruz, suffering his only defeat and losing an arm in the process.

The Canary Islands continued to develop as an important staging post on the route between Europe and South America, and then, possibly because of this constant exposure to visitors, eventually emerged as the major tourist centre they are today.

Statue Parque Municipal Santa Cruz (MR g5)

Places of Interest

Tenerife is a lot more than just a warm climate. Its society has been evolving for more than 400 years and the results can be seen in the cities, town and villages which are now scattered across the island. Each has something of interest for the visitor, while the countryside in between is endlessly fascinating with its dramatic countours and ever-changing scenery.

La Laguna *(MR* H2)

This is Tenerife's oldest city – home of the University of the Canary Islands and capital of Tenerife for 300 of the last 400 years – later supplanted by **Santa Cruz** *(MR* J2). You can still see some of the old academic buildings, dotted about the town, but the university itself is now housed in more modern, and less interesting, quarters a little away from the centre. This is a pleasant old town, with plenty of reminders of its glorious past. However, you would be well advised to park on the outskirts and do your sightseeing on foot, for its streets cannot really cope with the number of vehicles which attempt to pass through each day.

One of the long, narrow streets of the old town, *Obispo Rey Redondo*, contains at least three places which are worth visiting and most of the other interesting sights are only a short distance from it. At the bottom end is a pleasant square lined with some attractive old buildings – on one side, a covered market full of fruit, vegetables, meat, fish, fresh herbs and masses of colourful flowers – very typical of markets here and great fun to wander through.

A little further along is the *cathedral* (*MR* f7), seemingly under siege from the traffic which approaches it from all sides. Another unfortunate aspect is that someone decided to paint it pink – relieved, fortunately, by stone projections and topped by a sturdy round tower. But don't let the colour put you off – inside, once your eyes grow accustomed to the gloom, it is quite impressive – a church of calm, brooding dignity, dimly lit by high windows.

Five minutes walk along the same road will bring you to another religious building – this time painted an orange hue – the 16th century *Iglesia de la Concepcion* (Church of the Immaculate Conception). But, again, a visit is well rewarded, for this is one of the most beautiful churches in Tenerife.

Communications with **La Laguna** are excellent, with the motorway on its doorstep bringing **Santa Cruz** (*MR* J2) and **Puerto de la Cruz** (*MR* E3) within easy reach. And leading from it, down through the centre of the island, is what many consider the most attractive route of all – the road to Las Canadas (*MR* D5).

Botanical Gardens Puerto de la Cruz (MR n7)

Las Canadas (*MR* E6)

The journey from La Laguna is delightful: through pine forests, following the ridge of the mountain chain, allowing glimpses of first one shore and then of the other – sometimes both simultaneously. A little further on, at surprisingly high altitude, rich pastures appear complete with cows grazing – an unusual sight on Tenerife. Later, the scene becomes more rugged, relieved by mounds of yellow flowers squatting like giant yellow sponges on the floor of the desert and small conifers which dot the landscape. You can tell that you are approaching the area of the Las Canadas. On its outskirts, the crossroads of **El Portillo** (*MR* E5) offers welcome refreshment in the form of a restaurant and bar, with plenty of accommodation.

Los Roques (*MR* D6)

A few miles further on and the surroundings begin to take on the aspect of a lunar landscape: stretches of sand, rocks twisted into agonised shapes and lava everywhere, petrified in its headlong course down mountainsides or settled on the plains like some giant's ploughed field. On a nearby peak, gleaming white against the blue sky, the international observatory, in which Britain has an interest. And, then, eventually, the massive outcrop of rocks known as Los Roques. You can climb all over them and they provide an excellent vantage point from which to view the mountain and the surrounding countryside. Close by you will also find the Parador de las Canadas.

Mount Teide (*Pico de Teide*) (*MR* D5)

Famous as the highest point in Spain, this is also a really beautiful mountain, set amongst awe-inspiring scenery. To one side is a vast plain, flat like the bed of a lake, broken by jagged boulders, some pointing like fingers to the sky, ringed in the distance by sharp-edged rocks – a primeval landscape, which has been used to depict a prehistoric setting in at least one major film.

The easiest way to reach the peak is by cable car which runs each day between 09.00 and 16.00. This runs from a point near the road, starting out at 2356m/7000ft and travelling to a height of 3555m/11,000ft. People with any heart trouble are advised not to make the journey. When you emerge from the lift, you still have a little further to climb before reaching the summit. If the day is clear you will be rewarded with a magnificent view over the whole island and, possibly, of some of the other islands as well. The air up there is thin and can be quite cool, so take some warm clothes.

Landscape and Flowers Vilaflor (MR D7)

Vilaflor *(MR D7)*

After Teide, the road splits north and south, the southern
section heading down to Villaflor, 1500m/14,500ft above
sea level. This is a lovely town, typical of the best to be
seen in the Canaries – an agricultural centre where
oranges and lemons grow, surrounded by farmland and
vineyards. Well-tended flower beds line some of the
streets, making bright splashes of colour against the white
walls of the houses. Near the centre you will find a small
tree-lined square with a pretty church at one end. An
affluent town, it seems, seen at its best on the approach
road from across a ravine – every building clean and
white with red tiled roof. Some giant pine trees nearby are
an additional source of attraction.

Candelaria *(MR H4)*

The east coast motorway passes along the clifftops above
Candelaria so that, as you approach, the town is laid out
before you and you can look down and admire the
magnificent setting of the splendid *Basilica de Nuestra
Senora de la Candelaria* and the huge paved square
which adjoins it. The basilica, which houses a golden
statue of the Virgin Mary, patron saint of the archipelago,
takes up the whole of one side of the square with
buildings on two other sides and open to the sea on the
fourth. Along this open side is a series of 10 statues of the
Guanches (Tenerife's original inhabitants) – looking
somewhat weatherbeaten.

On one corner of the square there is a café where you
can sample some of the delicious tapas – small portions of
fish, meat, vegetables, and salad – which make such a
marvellous lunch, accompanied by a jug of the local
wine. Candelaria, nice enough already, will seem even
nicer after that.

Tacoronte *(MR G2)*

There are a number of places to visit around the north of
the island, all within easy reach of the main road. Some of
them are small and quiet, like the town of Tacoronte, with
no great pretensions to being a tourist attraction, but
interesting because they display another side of life on the
island. But this area does have other claims to fame, being
the main red wine producing region. And there are plenty
of bodegas or wine bars around where you can sample it.

La Orotava *(MR F3)*

Travelling westward along the same road will bring you to
La Orotava, one of the centres of lace-making, for which
the island is famous. The town is large, full of shops and
very busy – it's advisable to park as quickly as possible
and walk. A 15 minute uphill stroll from the centre of

Mount Teide (MR D5)

town will bring you to the *Avenida San Francisco* and the Casa de los Balcones, one of the places where lace is produced.

The lace is displayed in a grand old house, with balconies at every window, a cool, dark courtyard within shaded by bamboo trees and, on one side of it, carved wooden balconies on wooden pillars – almost mediaeval in appearance. In some of the rooms leading off, ladies in national costume work on the laces and in others there are shops where you can buy samples of their efforts.

Icod de los Vinos *(MR C4)*

Further west is Icod and the site of the famous 3,000 year old Dragon Tree *(Drago Milenaria)*. It is fascinating to speculate on what scenes the tree must have witnessed throughout those many years. The tree itself is like a giant, petrified mushroom, a gorgon's head with each outward curling snake ending in a prickly star. Above and behind it stands a small square, shaded by palm trees, leading to the pretty church of *Parroquia San Marcos* – outside, a tree-lined walk, bright red blooms and ornamental steps which rise towards white buildings with brown window frames and carved balconies so typical of Tenerife. From the terrace, you can look across the countryside and out over the sea.

Masca *(MR B5)*

The road continues as far as **Buenavista** (*MR* B4) and then heads south to **Santiago** (*MR* B5). There is a better road further east but the one we are taking goes through the hill village of Masca. The route is spectacular as it climbs higher and higher into the mountains and then begins to drop as it enters an enclosed valley. The road is steep and narrow and not for the faint-hearted, but take courage for the effort is worth it. There, clinging to the mountainside, are the tiny cottages which form the village – amidst a profusion of flowering cacti and brilliantly coloured flowers – no more than two or three rooms in each: flat roofs and small courtyards; a small goat tethered to a wall; an inquisitive dog peering round a corner; no roads, but rough, cobbled paths winding down amongst the houses; lower down, terraced plots of land descend to the valley below – and everywhere, lizards dart amongst the stones under the hot sun.

Nearby is a picnic spot – a favourite with the locals. Other paths lead to attractive viewpoints and some pretty restaurants, decked with flowers. And, from the road above, some of the most spectacular and dramatic views to be seen anywhere on the island.

Coastal Resorts

Tenerife has a fascinating coastline, full of surprises – long, rugged stretches, completely empty of people; some highly developed tourist playgrounds; and then, suddenly, a quiet fishing village almost untouched by the outside world. The road passes close to the shore throughout most of its length so that you can see, if not reach, nearly all of it. Quite a lot of it is inaccessible and, because tourism tends to be concentrated in certain areas, most of the coastline remains in its natural state, much of it very beautiful.

Clearly, the south coast holds the key to future tourist expansion. For, whilst the north is undoubtedly prettier, it is the south which can provide a more certain guarantee of that most desirable commodity – sunshine. The fastest growing resorts on the island are the southern duo of **Playa de Las Americas** (MR C8) and **Los Cristianos** (MR C8) which have the most superb facilities and the advantage of an airport nearby. This area is a convenient starting point for any survey of coastal resorts.

Almost a suburb of **Las Americas**, but now developing as a resort in its own right, **Torviscas** (MR C8) is a pleasant collection of hotels and apartments – nearly all with their own swimming pools – its own beach and an exceptionally well-designed marina. A relaxed atmosphere, a most attractive sea frontage and a wide choice of shops, bars and restaurants complete the picture. Immediately to the south is Playa de Las Americas, the island's busiest resort and almost certainly the liveliest place on Tenerife.

Next door, separated by a small headland, is **Los Cristianos**, a delightful resort with a busy harbour from which there are regular ferry sailings to the islands of **La Gomera** and **El Hierro** and boat trips to other parts of the coast. A long breakwater shelters a colourful mix of boats; small shops and restaurants crowd the waterfront; and cafés spread along the pedestrian walkway, with rows of tables and chairs throughout its length.

Just inland from Los Cristianos the motorway begins. This eventually loops up to **Santa Cruz** (MR J2) and **Puerto de la Cruz** (MR E3), but the first stop is **Costa del Silencio** (MR D8) and its smaller neighbour **Las Galletas** (MR D9). This is a new resort which really does live up to its name – a peaceful and relaxing place. Plenty of facilities with squash, tennis and golf course nearby.

A little further along, near the coast, is the airport (Aeropuerto Reina Sofia) and, just to the west of it, the tiny resort of **Los El Abrigo** (MR E8) – a mixture of old and new with some pleasant little eating places on the water's edge. Beyond the airport is one of the island's centres for wind-surfing, **El Medano** *(MR* F8). A wide bay and some good stiff breezes provide the ideal conditions.

The region we have just covered is the one where development is most intense. From here the motorway follows the coastline northwards passing a number of small beaches, but no towns of substance until **Candelaria** *(MR* H4) is reached more than half way up the east coast. However, this is better known for its cathedral than its beaches.

The motorway continues past a number of small coastal villages and onwards to **Santa Cruz** *(MR* J2). The inhabitants of the capital have, arguably, the island's most beautiful beach just a few miles up the coast – and it is almost entirely artificial. There, at **Playa de las Teresitas** *(MR* K2), is nearly a mile of golden sand – every grain of it brought from the Sahara. The effort was worth it, the result a complete success. It is a lovely beach, entirely natural in appearance. A lava stone breakwater creates a calm lagoon, safe for swimming. Palm trees give shade when needed.

Across on the north side of the island, near the eastern tip, there are three small villages close together, forming an attactive enclave – **Taganana** *(MR* J1), **Almaciga** *(MR* K1) and **Benijo** *(MR* K1) – remote and unspoilt, situated along a particularly attractive stretch of coast – no beaches, just a rocky shoreline. The fastest road west from here goes back through the mountains via La Laguna, past the other airport (Aeropuerto de los Rodeos) and heads for Puerto de la Cruz. On the way you will pass by **El Sauzal** *(MR* G2) a quiet, almost sleepy, town on the coast.

The road continues along the north coast through **Puerto de la Cruz** *(MR* G4) considered by many to be the oldest established tourist centre and most attractive town and coastal resort on Tenerife.

Luxury hotels, restaurants, plus excellent shopping facilities draw thousands of tourists here every week. The old harbour, with its small colourful fishing boats, is wel worth a visit. For those who wish to relax in the cool shade, then a visit to the Botanical Gardens is a must. Over a thousand species of plants from all over the world are on display here.

Most holidaymakers, however, are here for the sun, and there is no better place to bask and swim than Lake Martianez. The whole complex covers many acres with fresh and salt water pools, situated almost at sea level. The swimming is safe and there are also a number of good restaurants. Please note that there is an entrance fee.

And on to **Garachico** *(MR* F4) – a pleasant little village with a rocky shoreline. Its chief claim to fame is an old and tiny fort with a few rusting cannon, but more interesting are the church *Santa Ana* and the nearby

Convento de San Francisco (open 09.00-13.00, 16.00-19.00).

From **Garachico**, one branch of the road heads south via **Santiago** to the west coast at **Los Gigantes** (*MR* B5), famous for the range of dark steep cliffs which rise vertically out of the sea. It is also a delightful resort, beautifully laid out and, although new, already beginning to look quite mature; bright, neat and tidy with a smart marina, many hotels and villas and masses of flowers. **Puerto de Santiago** (*MR* B6) immediately adjacent to it follows the same pattern.

A series of attractive villages follow in succession down the western coastline, some of them developed as resorts, others remaining essentially unchanged. All are readily accessible since the road stays close to the coast almost as far as Playa de las Americas. **Alcala** (*MR* B6) is the first of these, a charming, unspoilt fishing village. Another very natural looking village, **San Juan** (*MR* B6) is less than 2 miles further south. A pleasant harbour with fishing boats and a huge breakwater, some restaurants and a tiny church in a raised square somewhat incongruously surrounded by a number of bars.

The tour of the coastline is completed with a small and comparatively new resort – **Callao Salvaje** (*MR* C7) – a mixture of hotels and apartments, some of them built into the cliffs; a small beach with a swimming pool and a restaurant built into the rocks with large picture windows giving a marvellous view of the sea below; there is, inevitably, a banana plantation nearby.

Los Roques (MR D6)

Santa Cruz de Tenerife

Santa Cruz is very much the capital of Tenerife – bigger, livelier and more impressive than any other town on the island. Here you will find the official buildings, the large squares, the museums, the concert halls and all the other signs of industry, commerce and culture that one associates with a major city. It is also a place of great charm – relaxing and undemanding, filled with interesting shops and some marvellous restaurants – playing host throughout the year to visitors from all over the world.

If you travel to Santa Cruz by car, then turn down onto the *Avenida Maritima*. This will bring you right through to the focal point of the town, the *Plaza de Espana*. If you are lucky, you will be able to park on the approach to the square or in the square itself. If not, there is a huge car park leading off from the right-hand side of the square as you approach it from the maritime route.

In Santa Cruz, all life, it seems, converges on the Plaza de Espana, a vast and attractive square, sited on the edge of the coast, with some splendid buildings on two sides, open-air cafes on a third and open on the fourth to the sea. A memorial to those who died in the Spanish civil war stands in the centre, the steps which lead up to it and the area around making a popular meeting point. Also popular as places to meet are the cafés and restaurants which take up most of the side furthest from the sea. Here you can sit in the sun and watch the world go by – always an entertaining pastime in such a cosmopolitan town as this – and plan your tour.

A good place to start is the tourist office which is in the *Palacio Insular*, a large building on the corner of the Plaza closest to the sea – always worth a visit for the detailed information on the island which they can give you. You will also find them extremely helpful in answering any questions you might have. Santa Cruz has many attractions and one of them is conveniently near – in fact, in the same building – the Archaeological Museum.

Archaeological Museum
(Museo Arqueologico Provincial)

No one could accuse the Tinerfenians of over publicising their past: the entrance to the museum is at the side of the building, through a narrow doorway and up two flights of stairs. But the effort is worth it, the charge minimal and you can learn a little about the tools and artefacts produced by the island's first inhabitants, the Guanches. Most interesting of all are the examples of mummified bodies – now little more than skeletons wrapped in leather and some form of matting. One room has hundreds of skulls in glass cases covering all four walls from floor to ceiling – a somewhat macabre exhibition. Flints and pottery from several of the islands are also displayed, as well as an old hand-operated mill from more recent times.

Church of the Immaculate Conception (*MR* h7)

When you leave the museum, turn left along the *Avenida de Bravo Murillo* (*MR* h7) and within a minute or two you will see on the right this rather neglected-looking church – *Iglesia Matriz de la Concepcion*. If it looks to be closed, there is a side entrance through which you can gain access. Inside, it appears anything but neglected, a really lovely church, beautifully proportioned with plain white walls, stained glass windows in muted colours and an ornate high altar with a statue of the Virgin as a centrepiece. To one side stands a graceful pulpit in marble, open-work beams and carved wood ceilings above and some elaborate side altars.

African Market *(Mercado Central)* (*MR* h7)

If you now carry on past the church and turn right up the *Avenida San Sebastian* (*MR* h7), 5 minutes' walk will bring you to what is known as the African Market or, more mundanely, the Mercado Central. Planted in a large open space at the junction of several roads, the arched entrance and clock tower of this colourful food market come constantly into view as one walks about the town. Wood carvings, probably African, are on sale at the entrance. Inside, flowers, fruit, vegetables and food of all kinds – even birds – are on display, some under cover, some open to the skies. If you want to buy food, then this is the place to get it. Alongside, there is another market – a long line of stalls selling clothing and gaudy gifts – good fun to wander through.

Parque Municipal Garcia Sanabria (*MR* g5)

Santa Cruz is not short of parks and open spaces. A straight road, *Valentin Sanz* (*MR* h6), extends from directly in front of the market to one of these – the *Plaza del Principe* – a quiet sheltered garden in which to relax for a moment. But be careful where you sit – the birds in the trees above are apt to make their presence felt in a most unsociable way. From here, it is quite a short walk up the *Calle del Pillar* (*MR* h6) to the Municipal Park, the largest in Santa Cruz, where exhibitions and concerts are occasionally held. The gardens are lovely with a wide range of statues, fountain displays, exotic trees and flowers, lots of cacti, and a huge flower clock which is illuminated at night.

The harbour (*MR* i6)

Retracing your steps to the Plaza de Espana (*MR* i6) will also bring you to the waterfront and the harbour, an endless source of interest where something is always happening. Claimed to be the busiest port in Spain, it plays host to ships from many different countries as they ply between Europe, Africa and the Americas. The jet foil to Las Palmas de Gran Canaria also sets off from here four times a day.

Puerto de la Cruz

The jewel of the north coast, Puerto de la Cruz (*MR* E3) is, even by the standards of this lovely island, something special. It is the island's tourist capital, a bright, bubbling place, attractively laid out – a place it is impossible not to enjoy. One of its attractions is that, while it is quite clearly a holiday centre, leaving no stone unturned in its attempt to satisfy the visitor's every need, these efforts have been imbued with a great deal of good taste. One has only to see the inspired design of the lido, that remarkable landscaped lagoon for sun worshippers, to appreciate how much care has been lavished on this most fortunate of tourist resorts.

The Lido (*MR* d1)

Puerto de la Cruz had no satisfactory beaches, just a rocky foreshore, so they simply created this 8-acre water park – the *Lago de Martianez* – a delightful series of individual pools and a huge ornamental lake, with islands and fountains to enliven the scene. Each day, people in their hundreds pour into the enclosure and relax in the sun, with everything they need close at hand – sunshine, crystal-clear water, bars, restaurants, reclining sunbeds and even first-aid facilities – safe for children and a joy for adults. Nearby is a gift market and artists who will paint your portrait. On the other side of the road, stylish hotels look down on the scene.

The Town

The town is a mixture of old and new – mostly new. A fishing village existed here before the tourists came and the old town remains as an attractive reminder of that past. Like Santa Cruz, it has its central meeting point, the *Plaza El Charco* (*MR* k6) – a large square with pleasant eating places, shaded by tall palm trees.

The old town with its narrow streets and traditional houses leads off from here – a pleasing contrast to the more modern sections. Nearby is the lovely 17th-century church of *Our Lady of La Pena de Francia* (*MR* l6) set in attractive grounds and well worth a visit.

Along the shore, near the fishing quarter, an open-air market sells leather goods, and fishing boats land their catches in a small sheltered harbour.

Elsewhere, food markets, shops in their thousands, wide pedestrian walkways, parks, restaurants, cafés, bars and, above all, the colourful mix of visitors combine to make this an exhilarating and memorable place. At night, there are clubs, discos, cinemas, flamenco dancing – in fact, entertainments of all kinds, including, in the *Parque de Taora* (*MR* 17), a luxurious casino – claimed to be one of Europe's finest. And, just outside the town, are some further attractions.

Botanical Gardens (*MR* n7)

Tenerife is itself a botanical garden, a paradise for the flower lover, where you can see the most remarkable plants growing in their natural habitat, with vibrant colours and strange shapes. Some of the more exotic ones are presented in these gardens, established 200 years ago – trees, shrubs and plants, not just from the Canary Islands but from all over the world. A small zoo adds to the pleasure.

Loro Parque

Claimed to be the largest collection of parrots in the world, this attractive park is home to more than 215 species, with most of them now breeding here successfully. Cranes, flamingos, cockatoos, macaws, humming birds, beavers, chimpanzees and, most recently, dolphins have been added to the menagerie. A very colourful display.

Bananera El Guanche

All you ever wanted to know about bananas but were afraid to ask. Bananera El Guanche provides you with a tour through a banana plantation – thousands of them, looking like small palm trees – and tells you all about their cultivation.

Zoolandia

A small zoo with lovely gardens and a small collection of animals including lions, tigers, cheetahs, bears, llamas and monkeys – all in cages – plus restaurant, bar and shops.

Touring by Car

Driving on Tenerife is a pleasant and not particularly taxing experience. The standard of driving is generally good and many of the roads are excellent. The road which circles the island is motorway or similar for two-thirds of its length and the remainder is of quite acceptable quality. The maximum permitted speed on this is 120 kpm/75 mph and then only for limited sections. Using this road alone will bring you within reach of all the major towns and coastal resorts. However, many of the towns were not designed to accommodate the motor car and even those that were sometimes find the volume indigestible. You will not have too much difficulty but, in the larger towns, it is better to park as soon as convenient and walk.

Seat belts must be worn when driving outside the towns. If you have not driven on the right-hand side of the road before, then take it very easily for a day or so. It is not difficult to acclimatise to the conditions, but a little time is needed in order to ensure that you do the right things automatically without having to think about them.

The most attractive roads are those which run inland and even these, though they twist and turn around the mountains and climb quite steeply in parts, are usually well surfaced. Most maps are reasonably accurate and provide a clear indication of each road's quality. The roads which lead to and from Mount Teide are amongst the most attractive on the island but there are others which, though lacking some of the more obvious scenic attractions, nevertheless have something to offer. One of these is the old road which runs down from **Santa Cruz** (*MR* J2) to **Los Cristianos** (*MR* C8).

It is an open road with some superb views and full of varied scenes, typical of the lives and habitats of the people away from the tourist areas. Since it is no longer the preferred route – the motorway now takes nearly all the traffic – it is likely to remain unaffected in the foreseeable future. The evening is the best time to make the journey – cooler, with less traffic about and the light at this time of day has a softening effect on the landscape. You can join the road at many different points – **Candelaria** (*MR* H4) is as good as any – and head south.

The road heads up into the hills towards **Güimar** (*MR* G4) but, instead of the direct route, it is worth making a short detour to take in **Arafo** (*MR* G4), a pleasant little village with a small square and a church – a mixture of old and new houses along the winding main street and a few bars. Then, a short distance away, Güimar – larger than Arafo, with the attractive parish church of *San Pedro Apostol*. The town has given its name to the valley which runs alongside, known for its production of white wine.

Tenerife
Photoguide.

A wide ranging collection of photographs of the area by professional photographers who also give you hints and tips on how to get the best from your holiday camera.

Introduction

For anyone who has ever taken a picture, there can be no finer location in the world than Tenerife. Within its compact dimensions, this island offers a quite outstanding display of colours and landscape, both natural and man-made.

Windsurfing at El Medano (MR F8)

Goat herd near La Orotava (MR F3)

Carnival Santa Cruz (MR J2)

The People

Although the original inhabitants of the island – the Guanches – have long since disappeared, the current population could hardly be more varied. The common language is Spanish, but people have settled here from Africa, Europe, Asia and the Middle East – thus ensuring a wealth of choice for the photographer. And they will have some marvellous photographic opportunities: on Tenerife it is customary to find fishermen, market traders, weavers, potters, embroiderers all practising crafts in public.

To capture the best in the local people, it's necessary to get into the countryside and seek them out in their own environment.

One of the best days for this is Sundays when the entire local population seems to pack up and leave home for a picnic or meal with an assortment of food and drink which they will gladly share with any photographer willing to take their photo.

Carnival Santa Cruz (MR J2)

Flower seller Santa Cruz Market (MR h7)

Banana plantation worker Sauzal (MR G2)

The Interior

Mount Teide (MR D5)

This must be the most exciting landscape throughout the Canaries. The park is really the natural volcanic crater of Mount Teide and is very important to Tenerife. For the photographer, it offers an unbelievable variety of terrain and colour. The highest points are bleak and desolate. Lower down are many pine woods. In the valleys, the famous banana plantations, citrus groves and vineyards flourish down as far as the coast.

Safari jeep Los Roques (MR D6)

Parador Las Canadas (MR D5)

Rock formations Los Roques (MR D6)

Holiday Glamour

An exotic beach is an ideal setting for pictures of glamour shots and when your wife or girlfriend is nicely tanned the results can look superb.

But remember, people's bodies are rather like their faces, they don't look their best when they are passive. Don't let your model just stand limply in front of the camera; encourage her to find a comfortable and flattering pose. It doesn't have to be the contorted manoeuvres used in the girlie magazines but your model's body does need to be positioned with a suggestion of movement so that it creates pleasing lines and flattering contours. Just asking her to put her hands up into her hair, for example, will raise and improve the bustline. A prop will be useful—a deckchair which she can stretch out in, or a windsurf sail which she can hold. Something quite natural is best for an inexperienced model. If none of these things are available, just kneeling on the sand or leaning on a rock can create quite pleasing poses.

Get in fairly close with the camera and fill the frame with your model. Choose an unobtrusive area—sea, sand or sky is ideal—or perhaps a textured reed sunbreak or beach hut.

If your model is tanned you can create a very pleasing effect using direct sunlight, but be careful to choose an angle which avoids ugly and obtrusive shadows. A little sun oil rubbed in well will give the skin a nice texture and make it appear even browner. For a professionally dramatic touch, flick some droplets of water onto the oiled skin and give half or one stop less exposure.

For a softer lighting effect, place your model in an area of shade or shoot into the light. For the latter it is important to give extra exposure as a reading taken into the light in the normal way will cause underexposure. Take a close up reading from the model herself, ensuring that the sunlight does not affect the exposure meter. With an automatic camera you can use the backlight button.

The Coast

Las Americas (MR C8)

Pirate Boat at Sea

Los Cristianos Harbour (MR d7)

Sea Pictures

The sea is an ideal subject for the camera. It has powerful visual qualities which can be used to create dramatic and atmospheric pictures. Because the colours and tones of the sea are very dependent upon the sky and the weather, they are constantly changing, offering a virtually limitless range of pictorial possibilities.

The Atlantic is a dramatic and changeable ocean and some care is needed to make it look its best. Remember that the strongest colour effect will be obtained when you are looking down at the sea from a high viewpoint when it is quite calm and wave-free. It is also best when the sky is a deep clear blue. Even when such optimum conditions prevail, you can improve the effect even further by using a polarising filter. By rotating the filter you can eliminate some of the light reflected from the water's surface, making it appear even more richly coloured.

However, the sea alone can be a little uninteresting, so it is best to look for other elements in the scene to create a focus of attention. Things which provide some contrast are most effective – a small boat or windsurfer with a bright sail, for instance, would provide a striking counterpoint to a deep grey-blue sea.

Foreground details will also add interest as well as helping to create an impression of depth and distance. Some boldly shaped rocks, for example or a cliff-side pine tree could be included close to the camera. Go for a wide angle lens for this type of picture to accentuate the perspective and further enhance the impression of depth. If you use a quite small aperture for maximum depth of field you should be able to get both the close foreground details and the distant scene equally sharp.

A final tip: don't leave your camera behind if the weather is stormy. Lowering dark clouds can make spectacularly impressive seascapes. You can take photographs with beautifully rich moody tones on days like these, especially just after a storm when the sunlight is beginning to break through the cloud. A degree of underexposure, half or one stop, will heighten the dramatic effect.

The Coast

Playa de las Teresitas (MR K2)

A trip around the coast of Tenerife offers the photographer as much variety as the rest of this remarkable island. There are a few disappointing moments – not even Tenerife is absolutely perfect! – but on the whole there is a wealth of different colours and textures to provide the ideal backdrop for the family album.

Las Americas Marina (MR a3)

Sunset

Garachico (MR C4)

Sunset Las Americas (MR C8)

Lido Puerto de la Cruz (MR d1)

To photograph some really spectacular sunsets, the place to be with your camera is Playa de las Americas, where the effect of the setting sun can have some very dramatic effects. Remember a degree of underexposure by half or one stop will heighten the pictures dramatic presentation.

Palms and Sea (MR d1)

Snapping up the Bargains

Beachlife is not the only kind there is. One of the most fascinating sights for the visitor is the local market, a glimpse into other people's everyday living. Whether it is a simple country market of local produce held in a village square or a busy city market with everything under the sun on display, it will provide an enjoyable morning for both shopping and sightseeing.

It is also a marvellous place to take photographs, particularly if you like to take spontaneous pictures of people. It is always much easier to photograph people when they are occupied in some way. In fact, a market gives you the best of both worlds: plenty of activity and a lively and relaxed atmosphere.

If you want to shoot unobserved – the candid camera approach – try to be as inconspicuous as possible. Don't carry your equipment in an obviously 'photographic' bag and keep your camera out of sight until the moment you want to take your shot. Try some shots with a long-focus lens; this will let you get quite close-up shots of people without having to hover about next to them and kill the

Playa de las Americas (MR C8)

spontaneity. Alternatively, pack a wide-angle lens; then you can shoot at very close quarters to your subject while making it appear that you are in fact photographing something beyond them.

Choose your viewpoint carefully, so that the background is as unobtrusive as possible. It will also give your pictures more impact if you frame the image quite tightly, and making sure that any distracting details are excluded. A market can be quite chaotic and you need to keep your pictures as simple and direct as possible.

For this reason it is also important to check that the lighting isn't too contrasty. If your shot includes large areas of both deep shade and bright sunlight, then you will get harsh unattractive pictures with very little detail. On a sunny day when the stalls are shaded by umbrellas or awnings, choose your viewpoints and frame your picture with care, so that the subject is either mainly in the shade *or* in the sunlight and set your exposure accordingly.

'North Coast'

Although there are some pleasant little villages on the north cape, the outstanding area on this side of the island must be Puerto de la Cruz. At the bottom of the beautiful Orotava Valley, it is hardly surprising that this town has grown to be such a popular resort. Again, it is impossible to list every worthwhile sight: much of the town itself, especially the old quarter – with its open markets, colonial houses and little streets – offers a wealth of photographic opportunity.

Los Cristianos Beach and Harbour (MR d7)

Church at Candelaria (MR H4)

Beach Puerto de Santiago (MRB6)

Fishermen La Caleta (MR B4)

Beach Playa de la Teresitas (MR K2)

'Off to Santa Cruz'
The road or motorway from
the south-west up to Santa
Cruz – the capital of Tenerife –
is probably the least
interesting part of our tour.
There are a few small fishing
villages, such as Roque de
Fasnia and Puerto de Guimar.
Most notable is Candelaria
with its famous church built
very close to the sea. A
definite place to stop and
snap.

Mountain Road Near Masca (MR B5)

Church Near La Guancia (MR D4)

Botanical Gardens Puerto de la Cruz (MR n7)

Harbour Santa Cruz (MR i6)

Tenerife's almost endless variety of colours, plants, wildlife and historic buildings (not to mention Mount Teide!) combined with its blue skies and bright sun, offers everyone – from the keenest photographer to the occasional snapper – a veritable paradise to explore with your camera.

Photohints

Shooting on the Seashore

The seashore is a particularly enticing subject for the photographer, but pictures taken by the sea can often be disappointing. One of the main reasons for this is faulty exposure. The brilliant light and reflective surroundings such as sea and sand, can mislead the camera's exposure meter into giving less exposure than is really needed, producing pictures which are dark, flat and dull. Overcome this by aiming your camera at a medium tone in the scene (shielding it from bright highlights) while you take an exposure reading. If you have an automatic camera, use the 'backlight' button or the exposure compensation dial set to +1 or +1½ stops.

Pictures by the sea are also often too blue, especially when you are using colour transparency film. There is a great deal of ultra violet light by the sea; although it is invisible to the eye, it creates a blue cast in film. Cure this by using a 'warm' lens filter, such as an 81A or 81B.

You could also try a polarising filter, a neutral grey filter which, when rotated, eliminates much of the reflected light in the scene. This makes blue skies a much deeper and richer colour and the sea appear more translucent.

Don't forget that while a beautiful expanse of sea may look delightful while you're there, in a photograph it can be very uninteresting. Look for something not too far from the camera to attract the eye, such as a fishing boat, or a windsurfer. This will also give your picture a sense of scale. Alternatively, find some foreground details to place close up to the camera—a palm tree, for example, or some flowers. This will frame the scene, making your picture more dramatic and creating an impression of depth and distance.

Finally, don't just stick to views and distant shots. There is much of interest on the seashore which can make even better pictures when taken close up. Rocks and rippled water for example, sun umbrellas, painted boats, fishing nets and lobster pots can all be used to make bold and colourful pictures when you move in closer to them.

Icod (MR C4)

Masca (MR B5)

New Arona (MR D7)

A little further on, as the road veers towards the coast, is the *Mirador de Don Martin (MR* G5), a viewpoint from which to admire the surrounding countryside, looking down on the Güimar Valley and the adjacent coastline. Traffic speeds along the motorway below. The road then continues on a parallel course, twisting and turning along the contours of the hillside, but always remaining in sight of the sea. The bends are very tight in places but the surface, with the exception of a few short stretches, is excellent. Lizards occasionally dart out, intent on making a hazardous crossing of the road, darting back just as quickly at the sound of a car – and, here and there, signs that they were not always successful.

A succession of tiny villages follows at frequent intervals, some just a collection of houses, attractive in their simplicity. No signs of any tourist interest here – hardly a café or restaurant to be seen, just a local bar or two. The next major point en route is **Granadilla de Abona** *(MR* E7), a traditional agricultural town, where refreshment can be found in its narrow streets. From here, there is a choice of two routes, one continuing in a similar fashion to **Los Cristianos** *(MR* C8), the other heading straight down to the motorway and a fast journey back to your starting point.

Rules of the Road

★ Drive on the right
★ Give way to traffic coming from the right, unless otherwise indicated
★ Seat belts must be worn
★ Do not exceed 120kpm/75mph on the motorway – slower on other roads
★ Carry your insurance papers with you

When to Go

Tenerife has one of the most beautiful climates in the world – consistently warm throughout the year, sometimes very warm indeed – so your choice of when to go will probably be determined more by circumstances at home than by conditions on the island. High season is when Britain is having its winter, the most popular period being Christmas. Prices are highest then but also rise and fall at other times of the year, such as Easter and peak British holiday periods.

Temperatures do vary from month to month, but not very dramatically, so that the highest maximum average in winter is similar to the lowest minimum average in summer. The countryside is probably at its most colourful in April and May, but flowers bloom throughout the year.

Average temperatures as supplied by the Spanish Meteorological Office:				
	Maximum		Minimum	
	F	C	F	C
January	68	20	58	14
February	70	21	58	14
March	72	22	59	15
April	74	23	61	16
May	76	24	63	17
June	79	26	66	19
July	83	28	68	20
August	84	29	70	21
September	83	28	70	21
October	79	26	66	19
November	75	24	63	17
December	70	21	61	16

How to Get There

Air

The majority of people travel to Tenerife by air, arriving at *Aeropuerto Reina Sofia (MR* E8), near the southern tip of the island. Scheduled flights operate from Heathrow but a high proportion of holidaymakers take charter flights, which are available at much reduced rates from a large number of British airports.

Direct flights can also be made from many other European centres and there are daily flights between Tenerife and the islands of Lanzarote, Fuerteventura, Gran Canaria, La Palma and El Hierro. These land at *Aeropuerto de los Rodeos* or *Aeropuerto Tenerife-Norte, the domestic airport* (*MR* H2).

Sea

The shortest sea route to Tenerife is the liner service which runs from Cádiz in southern Spain via Las Palmas on alternate days from June to mid-October and thereafter six times a month. It docks at **Santa Cruz** (*MR* J2). It is also possible to travel direct from Southampton. You will need to check with your travel agent as to which shipping lines operate a service.

Insurance

It is certainly advisable to take out travel insurance – the cost is low and you can obtain cover for a wide range of possibilities. Your travel agent will be able to offer you some schemes and you can also check with your insurance broker. Prices vary and so does the cover, so shop around and check the small print. Some place severe restrictions on their coverage of money loss.

You should be able to obtain cover for the following:

★ Medical expenses
★ Hospital benefit
★ Personal accident
★ Death
★ Loss of property, including money
★ Personal liability
★ Unavoidable cancellation of, or delay in, travel arrangements
★ Cost of return flight should you miss the plane.

Passport and Customs

You must have a passport, but British citizens do not need a visa.

Prices for many items are much lower in Tenerife than in Britain – for example, there is no point in taking alcohol and cigarettes with you.

When it comes to alcohol, Spanish-produced drinks offer the best value – Spanish gin and brandy are particularly cheap. There are also some excellent wines but the savings are much less and there is a limit to the number of bottles you can reasonably carry back with you.

Know Your Limit

When you tear yourself away from Tenerife, this is what you can take with you, provided you are over 18:

200 cigarettes OR 50 cigars OR 250g tobacco
1½ litres of spirits AND 2 litres table wine

You can of course take more, but you will have to pay duty on them.

Food and Drink

You can eat well almost anywhere in Tenerife, but in the main resorts the menu will tend to be orientated towards the British palate in particular and European tastes in general. However, there are many places, particularly in the north of the island, where you can sample some of the dishes which are peculiar to Tenerife or, at least, Spanish in origin.

As a starter, the avocados take some beating. They are quite superb here and are delicious served with prawns.

Tapas, those enticing bite-sized morsels, make an ideal lunch, particularly when washed down with local wine or beer. But this is quite a pricey way of eating, so be careful.

Roast sucking pig (*lechona*) a Segovian speciality, is also popular in Tenerife.

Some tasty local dishes to try out on your taste buds include:

Viejas – white fish boiled with salted potatoes

Conejo en Sarmorejo – rabbit braised in white wine

Potaje de Berros – watercress soup with vegetables

Papas arrugadas con mojo – salted potatoes with spicy sauce

Puchero Canario – vegetable stew

For dessert, you must, of course, sample the island's basic commodity – bananas. You will find these served in a variety of ways. The banana split is usually quite generously proportioned, and fried bananas (*platanos fritos*) served dusted in sugar and sprinkled with brandy and fresh lemon juice are delicious. Children will like *bizcochitas de gofio*, a Canarian speciality, biscuits made from *gofio* (wheat or maize flour) and bananas.

The choice of drink is very wide, ranging from all manner of fruit juices through almost every type of alcohol. And the cost is not high, unless you choose something particularly exotic. There are some excellent Spanish wines such as Rioja, well known in Britain. There are also many local wines which are certainly not as good but, nevertheless, are well worth sampling. For their price, which is very low, they can be excellent value and a pleasant accompaniment to any meal. Both red wine *(tinto)* and white *(blanco)* are made on Tenerife.

Telephone (*Telefono*)

There are public telephones in all the towns and resorts on the island, as well as in restaurants, bars and hotels. You can make local calls on any of these.

International calls can be dialled direct from telephone boxes marked Telefono Internacional. These are efficient push-button systems with a sloping channel into which you can place up to six or seven coins at a time, each one falling automatically into the slot as required by the length of the call. The boxes take 5, 25 and 100pta coins. 5pta will only serve for local calls. For international calls, you will need about four or five 100pta coins at least, so have these lined up ready.

Phoning from hotels, although more convenient, can be much more expensive and it is well worth learning how to use a public phone.

How to Phone Home

★ dial 07
wait for the dialling tone to rise to a steady, sharper pitch
★ dial 44 – the international code for Britain
★ dial the area code but omitting the zero
(for example, for London dial 1 only)
★ then dial the rest of the number as normal

Postal Services (*Correos*)

It has to be admitted that the postal service from Tenerife is not the world's fastest and if you do not send off your postcards within the first day or two, the chances are they will arrive after your return home. You can buy your stamps from hotel receptions and from wherever you buy your cards.

Accommodation

Hotel accommodation ranges from one to five star classification. On a lower scale than this are the *Hostals*, smaller family-run hotels which are graded from one to three stars. What you can expect under each category is listed by the Spanish National Tourist Office. All hotels and hostals are obliged to provide you with the amenities appropriate to their star rating.

Toilets

The only public toilets, with one or two exceptions, are those found in bars, hotels and restaurants. They are free, but if there is an attendant present, a small tip (25-30 ptas) is always welcome.

Electricity (*Electicidad*)

The electricity supply is 220 V throughout the island so you will be able to use your electric appliances without adjustment. You will also need a continental two-pin adaptor (fairly easy to obtain on Tenerife) to fit the electrical sockets. The British two-pin is not suitable.

Water (*Agua*)

The water is purer than on the mainland of Spain and probably all right to drink. Certainly, the islanders drink it. Nevertheless, if your stomach is easily upset, or you would just rather play safe, then it is better to stick to the bottled variety (*agua minerals*) which you can buy in bars, shops and supermarkets all over the island. It is available *con gas* (with bubbles) or *sin gas* (without) – much cheaper in litre bottles or larger.

Holiday Reading

There is no shortage of paperbacks – all the resorts have large quantities of them – usually of the lighter variety, although there are some serious bookshops in the larger towns. Prices, however, are nearly double those in Britain.

British newspapers are widely available, although one or two days late. English language papers are also published on Tenerife:

* *Here and Now* – weekly newspaper
  Island Gazette – monthly magazine in colour
* *Canarian News* – weekly tabloid

(* *Including overseas news.*)

You will find these papers in a variety of places – some of them in paper shops and on magazine stands and others in hotel lobbies and supermarkets. The Spanish for newspaper is *périodico*.

Photography

The light on Tenerife is so good and the scenery so enchanting that with only a little effort you can produce some shots of real beauty. Certainly, it is the sort of place that can bring out the best in you, photographically speaking.

Film is relatively cheap on Tenerife, so it is probably better to bring just a small quantity with you to start off with and then buy the remainder there. The Spanish word for film is *carrete: en blanco y negro* for black and white; *para película en color* for colour and *de diapositivas* for colour slide film.

If you are in a hurry to see your pictures, then there are many places offering processing within a few hours.

Weights & Measures

Metric units have been in use in Britain for some time now but, for those more familiar with imperial measurements, the following conversion tables may be of some help. The figures are approximate.

Weight

1 lb	= 0.45 kilo (kg)
2 lb	= 0.9 kilo
2.2 lb	= 1 kilo

Roughly speaking, if you buy half a kilo of food, you will get just over a pound in weight.

Length

12 inches	= 30 cm
40 inches	= 1 metre
0.62 mile	= 1 kilometre
1 mile	= 1.6 kilometres

Liquids

1 pint	= 0.6 litre
1.8 pints	= 1 litre
1 gallon	= 4.6 litres

Sizing Up

The following table may help you find the correct dress and shoe size, but remember that sizes vary from maker to maker, just like home.

Women's Clothing

UK	Spain/Tenerife
10	40
12	42
14	44
16	46
18	48

Women's Shoes

UK	Spain/Tenerife
3	35
4	36
5	37
6	38
7	39

Men's Clothing

UK	Spain/Tenerife
36	46
38	58
40	50
42	52
44	54

Shirts

UK	Spain/Tenerife
14	36
14½	37
15	38
15½	39
16	40

Men's Shoes

UK	Spain/Tenerife
6	40
7	41
8	42
9	43
10	44

Money Matters

The unit of currency is the peseta (pta), available in the following denominations:

Coins: 1, 5, 10, 25, 50, 100, 200 pesetas

Notes: 100, 200, 500, 1000, 2000, 5000, 10,000 pesetas

You may take any amount of foreign currency into Tenerife, whether in notes or travellers' cheques, but may take out no more than 100,000 pesetas in Spanish currency or up to the equivalent of 500,000 pesetas in foreign currency, unless you previously declared the excess amount at Customs when arriving on the island.

You don't need to get Spanish money before leaving the UK, unless you want to spend some en route. Travellers' cheques, with a guarantee of replacement if lost, are much safer and many places, such as hotels, department stores and the larger shops and restaurants, will accept one or more of the major credit cards, e.g.:

★ Mastercharge (Access)
★ Eurocard
★ Visa (Barclaycard, Trustcard, etc)
★ American Express
★ Diners Club

But, of course, it is best to check on this before you buy.

Many shops and hotels will also accept travellers' cheques either for exchange into Spanish currency or as direct payment, but the best rate of exchange is obtained from a bank. Whenever you are changing money, take your passport with you as proof of identity.

The rate of exchange is constantly changing, so always check up on it before you cash your cheques. Alternatively, get your travellers' cheques in pesetas; when you change them you will receive the amount stated on each, without having to worry about the rate of exchange.

Banking Hours

There are plenty of banks in all the major towns and resorts.

09.00–14.00 Monday–Friday
09.00–13.00 Saturday

Take your passport with you for any transaction.

Police (*Policía*)

There are three police forces on Tenerife:

Guardia Municipal

Local police, wearing blue uniforms with blue hats – responsible for local traffic, parking etc. in towns.

Guardia Civil

National police force wearing green uniforms with black patent leather hats – concerned with airport control and highway patrols (checking speeding and other motoring offences).

Policía Nacional

A national anti-crime force who wear beige jackets with brown trousers and hat.

All three forces carry guns.

The police are extremely helpful to tourists and you can approach any of them if you need assistance. However, the Guardia Civil are the ones most likely to speak English.

Robbery

If you have anything stolen then report this immediately to the nearest police station. A statement will be taken and, if you have lost documents such as passport, driving licence etc, they will give you a certificate to that effect, which will assist you during your stay – for example when changing money – but will not do as a substitute passport for your return home. For that you will need to contact the British Consul (*MR* h6) (*Suárez Guerra, 40-5th Edifico Marichal, Santa Cruz, tel: 24 20 00*). Open Monday–Friday 10–12).

Medical Help

There is no shortage of medical assistance at all the major resorts throughout the island. Medical centres are clearly identified with a bright red cross on a white background and chemists (*farmacias*) have a green cross to advertise themselves.

Tenerife's General Hospital (tel: 21 75 11) is only a short distance outside **Santa Cruz**, just off the main road which runs to **La Laguna** (*MR* J2). There is a hospital in **Playa de Las Americas** (*MR* C8) (tel: 79 16 00). There are also many other smaller hospitals or clinical establishments at **Candelaria** (*MR* H4), **Los Cristianos** (*MR* C8), **Puerto de la Cruz** (*MR* E3), **Garachico** (*MR* C4), **Icod de los Vinos** (*MR* C4), **La Laguna** (*MR* H2), **Los Llanos** (La Palma Island) and **La Orotava** (*MR* F3). And there are several more within Santa Cruz itself.

Before leaving Britain, pick up Form E111 from your local DHSS. If you fill this in and take it with you, it entitles you to free medical treatment in Spain and all other common market countries, but not, of course, to free medicine.

Island Transport

There is no railway on Tenerife and so the only means of getting about the island is by road. You have the choice of scheduled bus service, excursion coach, taxi or hired car. Motorbikes, mopeds and bicycles may also be hired in some tourist centres. Hitch-hiking is attempted by quite a few and appears to meet with reasonable success.

Buses

An extensive network of bus services crisscrosses the island. Opinions vary as to how reliable these are but there are substantial numbers of them running between the main centres, and they do provide a very cheap form of transport. Timetables change so you will need to check at one of the bus stations. A large proportion of the routes start out from **Santa Cruz** *(MR J2)*, with bus stations at the *Plaza de Espana* (MR i6) and *Calle Tome Cano* (MR f8), and from **La Laguna** *(MR H2)* at the *Plaza de San Cristobal*. More information can be obtained from the inter urban bus transport offices at **Poligono Industrial Costa Sur**, tel. 21 80 55 and 21 84 55.

Each of the larger towns also has its own local bus service.

Tourist Buses

Several special bus tours run from **Santa Cruz** and from **Puerto de la Cruz**. These take in such areas as **Las Canadas** *(MR D5)*, **La Orotava** *(MR F3)* and the southern coastal resorts.

Taxis

There is no shortage of these in all the main towns and resorts. All have meters and for normal journeys the price will follow a set scale of charges. If you want to use a taxi for an excursion – quite reasonable if there are three or four of you – then you will need to negotiate a price *before* you set out.

Car Hire

While you can see much of the island using public transport, a private car gives you much greater flexibility, and a freedom of movement unmatched by other means.

Finding a car hire company will not be one of your problems – each resort has several, sometimes dozen and you will find them at the airports as well – but prices vary, so shop around. The price is in three parts: the basic hire charge, VAT and insurance. You will also be charged for a full tank of petrol and be expected to return the car with the tank full. Spanish for petrol is *gasolina*.

Sea Routes

With the exception of Gomera, all the islands can be reached by air. However, the sea journey is an adventure in itself and a pleasant change from air travel.

The following are the main routes:

Tenerife ⬦ Gran Canaria
Santa Cruz – Las Palmas
Monday, Thursday, Friday and Sunday (1 departure)
Tuesday, Wednesday and Saturday (2 departures)

Gran Canaria ⬦ Tenerife
Las Palmas – Santa Cruz
Wednesday, Thursday and Sunday (1 departure)
Monday, Tuesday, Friday and Saturday (2 departures)

Tenerife ⬦ Fuerteventura ⬦ Lanzarote
Santa Cruz – Puerto del Rosario – Arrecife
Tuesday, Thursday and Sunday (1 departure)

Tenerife ⬦ Lanzarote
Santa Cruz – Arrecife
Monday, Wednesday, Friday, Saturday and Sunday

Lanzarote ⬦ Tenerife
Arrecife – Santa Cruz
Monday, Wednesday, Thursday and Sunday

Fuerteventura ⬦ Tenerife
Puerto del Rosario – Tenerife
Tuesday, Thursday and Saturday

Tenerife ⬦ La Palma
Santa Cruz de Tenerife – Santa Cruz de la Palma
Monday, Thursday and Friday

La Palma ⬦ Tenerife
Santa Cruz de la Palma – Santa Cruz de Tenerife
Tuesday, Thursday and Saturday

Tenerife ⬦ Gomera ⬦ Hierro
Los Cristianos – San Sebastian – Valverde
Monday and Friday

Hierro ⬦ Tenerife
Valverde – Tenerife
Wednesday and Friday

Tenerife ⬦ Hierro
Los Cristianos – Valverde
Monday, Tuesday, Wednesday and Friday

Tenerife ⬦ Gomera
Los Cristianos – San Sebastian
Monday, Tuesday and Friday

Gomera ⬦ Tenerife
San Sebastian – Los Cristianos
Monday, Wednesday and Friday

Quite apart from the above, there is also the Ferry Gomera which runs twice daily from **Los Cristianos** (*MR* C8) at 10.00 and 20.00 hours. The journey to San Sebastian de Gomera (see Gomera Island) takes 1 hour 15 minutes.

Useful Words & Phrases

You will certainly be able to make your way around using only English, since it is widely spoken throughout the tourist areas. Nevertheless, it is always worth trying to learn a few Spanish phrases – and there are occasions, particularly if you find yourself off the beaten track, when the knowledge could be useful.

Yes	Si
No	No
Please	Por favor
Thank you	Gracias
Good morning	Buenos dias
Good afternoon	Buenas tardes
Good evening	Buenas noches
Hello	Hola
Goodbye	Adios
I don't understand	No comprendo
How much is that?	Cuanto es eso?
What?	Que?
Why?	Por que?
Where?	Dónde?
When?	Cuándo?
How many?	Cuantas?
Do you speak English?	Habla Ingles?
Good	Bueno
Bad	Malo
I would like . . .	Quisiera . . .
What time is it?	Que hora es?
I don't speak Spanish	No hablo Espanol
Open	Abierto
Closed	Cerrado
Big	Grande
Small	Pequeño
Hot	Caliente
Cold	Frio
Very	Muy
Today	Hoy
Tomorrow	Mañana
Left	Izquierda
Right	Derecha
Waiter/Waitress!	Camerero/camerera!
The bill please	La cuenta, por favor
Travellers cheques	Cheques de viaje
I want to change (currency)	Quiero cambiar (libras)
Is this the road for . . .?	Es esta la carretera hacia . . .?
Fill the tank please	Llénolo, por favor
May I take a photograph?	Puedo sacar una fotografia?
I have lost my . . .	He perdido mi . . .
Help!	Socorro!

Los Roques (MR D6)

Sport & Entertainment

Tenerife has plenty of sport to satisfy even the most active. Swimming, of course, is the most common of all and, for this, there are beaches along all its shores and literally thousands of swimming pools of all shapes and sizes – the majority of them belonging to groups of apartments, villas, hotels and various sports complexes.

Entertainment too is plentiful in all its variety both during the day and in the evening.

Golf

There is an 18-hole course at *Golf Club El Penon* near **Los Rodeos** airport *(MR H2)* and 2 other courses, Amarillo and Golf del Sur, close to Reina Sofia airport.

Mini-golf can be played at:

Parque Garcia Sanabria, **Santa Cruz** *(MR g5)*
Ten-bel, **Las Galletas** *(MR D9)*
Club de Tenis Punta del Rey, **Las Caletillas** *(MR H4)*

Tennis

Every resort has large numbers of tennis courts, many of them as part of hotel and private complexes but these and others generally available for hire.

These are some of the clubs:

Club Malibu, **Tabaiba, El Rosario** *(MR H3)*
Outdoor Games Club, **Puerto de la Cruz**
Club Atalaya, **La Laguna** *(MR H2)*
Oceanic Tennis Club, **Puerto de la Cruz**
Club El Roque, **Garachico** *(MR C4)*
Club de Tenis Punta del Rey, **Las Caletillas** *(MR H4)*
Las Arenitas, **Las Caletillas** *(MR H4)*
Club Nautico La Galera, **Candelaria** *(MR H4)*
Circulo Amistad XII de Enero, **Candelaria** *(MR H4)*

Windsurfing

El Medano *(MR F8)* is the centre for this, a pleasant open beach and good conditions for windsurfing.

Surfboarding

Not quite up to Hawaii standards but conditions, particularly off **Playa de las Americas** *(MR C8)* are good enough to tempt a fair number to try their skills.

Skin Diving

Clear water and an indented coastline provide plenty of interest and ideal conditions for skin diving. There is a skin-diving school at *Escuela de Bucco*, Fernandez Herrero 11, **Santa Cruz** *(MR g7)*.

La Guancia (MR D4)

Water Skiing

Puerto de la Cruz (*MR* E3) and **Playa de las Americas** (*MR* C8) and other southern resorts, in particular, are popular locations for water skiing.

Horse Riding

A number of stables have horses available – check at the local tourist office for details.

Judo

Judo is practised at the following:

Karate-Judo, Calle Numancia, **La Laguna** (*MR* h2)

Anaterve Vilar, General Godet 85, **Santa Cruz** (*MR* f6)

Hotel Bougainville, **Playa de las Americas** (*MR* b3)

Clay-pigeon Shooting

Le Mesa Mota, **La Laguna** (*MR* H2)

Fishing

Fishing is popular all round the coast but you need a licence, available from *Servicio de Pesca*, Jefatura Regional de Icona, Avenida de Anaga, **Santa Cruz** (*MR* i6).

Spectator Sports

Football, wrestling and basketball are popular sports and you will be able to see these at a number of venues during the appropriate seasons.

Walking/Hiking

Tenerife offers the dedicated walker a wonderfully varied countryside in which to wander. If you are really keen then you cannot do better than buy the beautifully illustrated pocket guide *Landscapes of Tenerife* by Noel Rochford, published by Sunflower Books and available in English bookshops as well as those in Tenerife. This gives maps and precise details for 5 car tours and 60 long and short walks, as well as picnic locations for the less intrepid.

Parque Municipal (MR g5)

Excursions

Half-day and whole-day excursions are organised to:

Las Canadas del Teide
Santa Cruz and **La Laguna**
Orotava Valley
Icod and **Garachico**
Masca, Arafo and **Adeje**
Island Tour

These depart from a number of points. For details check at the tourist office.

There are also a number of night-time excursions leaving from **Puerto de la Cruz**, **Bajamar** and from **Playa de las Americas**.

Casino Taoro (*MR* 17)

Situated in beautiful gardens in **Puerto de la Cruz**, this is claimed to be Spain's finest casino.

Winter opening:

Sunday to Thursday	20.00–03.00
Friday	20.00–04.00
Saturday	20.00–05.00

Summer opening:

Sunday to Friday	21.00–04.00
Saturday	21.00–05.00

A new casino is planned for **Playa de la Americas**. In the interim, gaming facilities are available in the Hotel Tinerfe.

Burro Safari

Donkey rides through the countryside variously described as taking place at **Arafo** (*MR* G4) or **Candelaria** *(MR H4)*. In fact, you will find them somewhere between the two on the road to **Araya** *(MR* E4). Probably easier to take one of the excursion coaches which bring people here. Beautiful countryside.

Zoos & Gardens

Loro Parque
Claimed to be the world's largest collection of parrots

Banana Plantation
Acres of bananas and a guided tour

Zoolandia
Small and attractive zoo

Botanical Gardens (*MR* n7)
Exotic display of plants

Lido Martianez (*MR* m5)
Acres of landscaped swimming pools.

More information on the above can be found under Puerto de la Cruz, p.41.

Fishing Boats (MR d7)

Festivals, Fairs & Festivities

The Carnival

The biggest annual festivity in Tenerife is the Carnival, claimed to be second only to the one that takes place in Rio de Janeiro. Full of colour and lively activity this runs during the two weeks leading up to Lent. Although things are happening all over the island, the main centres of activity are **Santa Cruz** (*MR* J2) and **Puerto de la Cruz** (*MR* E3), with **Icod de los Vinos** (*MR* C4) also playing an important part. A marvellous spectacle.

Fiestas de Mayo

Throughout May, in Santa Cruz, there are flower displays, handicraft, folk activities, opera and theatre. These begin during the feast of the Holy Cross (Santa Cruz) at the beginning of the month.

Romerias

Very popular folklore festivals which take place on a few feast days in certain towns.

Los Realejos (*MR* E3) 15th May – feast in honour of San Isidro and Santa Maria de la Cabeza

Orotava del Corpus (*MR* F3) June (date not fixed) – carpets of flowers and Romeria de San Isidro Labrador – also in La Orotava

La Laguna (*MR* H2) – Romeria de San Benito

Garachico (*MR* C4) 16th August – Romeria de San Roque

Music Festival

The actual dates vary but this feast of music starts about the second week in January and continues until the first week in February. During this period, musicians of international renown perform each day at the *Teatro Güimera*, a delightful baroque theatre in **Santa Cruz** (*MR* h7). Visitors have included the London Symphony Orchestra, the Berliner Oktett, the Melos Quartet Stuttgart and the Hamburg Symphony Orchestra.

Concerts

The Tenerife Symphony Orchestra gives concerts on Friday evenings at two-week intervals in the *Teatro Güimera* (*MR* h7). The season lasts from September until the end of June. The orchestra is remarkably well disciplined and provides a marvellous evening's entertainment at a ridiculously low price.